W9-AWB-848

THEN & NOW

BALTIMORE ARCHITECTURE

Charles Duff and Tracey Clark
on behalf of the
Baltimore Architectural Foundation

Copyright © 2006 by Charles Duff and Tracey Clark
ISBN 978-0-7385-4281-2

Library of Congress control number: 2006923075

Published by Arcadia Publishing
Charleston, South Carolina

Printed in the United States of America

Then and Now is a registered trademark and is used under license from
Salamander Books Limited

For all general information contact Arcadia Publishing at:
Telephone 843-853-2070
Fax 843-853-0044
E-mail sales@arcadiapublishing.com
For customer service and orders:
Toll-Free 1-888-313-2665

Visit us on the Internet at www.arcadiapublishing.com

ON THE FRONT COVER: These views of the skyline of Baltimore looking west from Broadway shows the heart of the city in the 1930s and today. At first glance, the houses in the foreground may appear to have changed less than the skyscrapers in the distance. Look again. Almost all of the houses in the foreground of the modern picture were built in 2004 and 2005. The old houses in the 1930s view had disappeared by 1980, replaced by parking lots and a large hospital. Urban change is continuous but sometimes elliptical. (Courtesy of the Enoch Pratt Free Library.)

ON THE BACK COVER: Downtown Baltimore has been rebuilt many times. This picture catches the Victorian rebuilding of the Georgian city in mid-stride. The buildings at right are at least 50 years older than those at the corner. Buildings were smaller here than on more prominent streets but no less elaborate. (Courtesy of the Enoch Pratt Free Library.)

THEN & NOW

BALTIMORE
ARCHITECTURE

CONTENTS

Acknowledgments   vii

Introduction   ix

1.   Panoramas: The Official View and Other Views   11

2.   The Harbor: The Beginning, the Middle, the Apparently Endless   19

3.   Downtown: The Epicenter of Growth, Change, and the Occasional Catastrophe   27

4.   Westside: Much More Than the Retail Core   45

5.   North Central: Fashion Follows Charles Street   53

6.   Northwest: The Turbulent Seas around Bolton Hill   75

7.   Moving Out from the Center: Lost Worlds and Altered Landmarks   89

ACKNOWLEDGMENTS

The archives of Baltimore are rich and well staffed. Of inestimable value are the collections of photographs and books in the Maryland Department of the Enoch Pratt Free Library, under the more than capable stewardship of Jeff Korman. Jeff's stacks and tables became our second home and our second office. We are grateful for his tolerance and warmth as well as for his knowledge.

Mary Markey and the Maryland Historical Society have opened their collection to us. We are proud to display a tiny tip of that magnificent iceberg and delighted to acknowledge the expert help of Diertra Thompson. Andy Herbick has contributed a wonderful amount of time and photographic skill. Lauren Bobier, our editor at Arcadia, has given made it possible for us to order our enthusiasm and get the job done.

The history of Baltimore as a physical environment can be understood today largely through the work of volunteers in the Baltimore Architecture Foundation. This is a true community of scholars with the generosity of amateurs and, very often, the skill of professionals. Jim Wollon, the tireless and almost omniscient head of the foundation's research group, the Dead Architects' Society, has been as helpful with the specifics of this book as he has been, over the past decades, with every other aspect of the city's architectural history. Dr. Lance Humphries has put his unique knowledge of Georgian Baltimore at our disposal. We await his book with eagerness.

Each of us has family, colleagues, and friends to thank, both for tolerating our absences and for at least appearing to share our excitement. Lydia Duff is in a class by herself. Robert Duff, Trevor Hill, Colin Busch, Sarah Bentley, Andy Herbick, and David Kahan helped us to dodge meter maids and poked with us down some very strange alleys.

Finally the authors are grateful to each other. Our clear division of tasks melted away before we knew it, and each of us has helped the other on every aspect of this book. A happy collaboration has turned work into friendship.

INTRODUCTION

Baltimore is one of America's oldest and loveliest big cities. For almost 300 years, the people of Baltimore—a kaleidoscopic mix from the beginning—have been building and rebuilding their city. They have built some of America's greatest buildings and formed some of America's greatest urban and suburban environments. Now, after 50 tough years, Baltimoreans are beginning again to walk with a spring in their step. They are rediscovering their city, preserving what they like, changing what they dislike, and generally trying to make the city a proper stage for the play of their imagination.

This is Baltimore's normal condition. Baltimoreans have rarely been content to leave their city as they found it. As the community has grown, as tastes have changed, as business has evolved and technology advanced, Baltimoreans have built and razed buildings, opened and closed streets, and restored and demolished whole neighborhoods. Baltimore today is literally 10,000 times bigger than it was when our oldest picture was made in 1752. Change is one of the laws of urban life.

Baltimore is fortunate to have a wealth of surviving historic buildings and neighborhoods, but this book is not about them. This book is about change, and we have sought the places where urban and architectural changes have been most dramatic and most interesting, hence our concentration on the center of the city. The average piece of ground in downtown Baltimore has had seven buildings since 1730. That is an irresistible target for the student of urban change.

We hope that our method will not leave you with too many feelings of sadness. Because we started with archival images and picked them for the beauty of the scene or the shock value of the change, we may well give you the impression that all of Baltimore's changes have been for the worse. We do not believe this. If we had started with our favorite views in today's Baltimore and then matched them to archival images, we would probably give a more positive impression. Perhaps that will be our next book.

To get the sense of Baltimore, imagine a city halfway between London and Los Angeles. Founded in 1730, Baltimore was originally a British city. It remained British in architecture long after the Revolution, and many of the buildings and streetscapes in our book would look at home on either side of the North Atlantic. But each year has made the pull of London weaker and the pull of Los Angeles stronger. The long, straight streets of Baltimore's 1822 plan are American, as are the skyscrapers that have been the focus of architectural pride since the 1890s. Today the two forces are in a kind of equilibrium: new suburban development follows American patterns of sprawl, while a sudden burst of new urban development is making Baltimore's waterfront look and feel like the gentrified Thames east of the Tower.

In the meantime, here is Baltimore, then and now, an American city with an almost European density of architectural experience. We hope that our book will help you to feel that Baltimore belongs to you.

PANORAMAS

THE OFFICIAL VIEW AND OTHER VIEWS

VIEW FROM FEDERAL HILL, 1752. The official view of Baltimore is a view of Downtown from Federal Hill. Here is an engraved version of the oldest official view, a pencil sketch by John Moale in 1752. Baltimore was already 22 years old in 1752, but it was insignificant and gave no sign of future greatness. John Moale's Baltimore was still merely a typical Chesapeake village beside a swamp. Of its 25 houses, only two were built of brick. Note the gambrel roofs; these houses would not look out of place in Williamsburg. Baltimore's takeoff began just two years later, and this scene was unrecognizable within a decade. (Courtesy of the Maryland Historical Society.)

VIEW FROM FEDERAL HILL, 1850. Now a city of 167,000 people, Baltimore by 1850 had filled almost half of its original harbor and covered its hills with buildings. Classical monuments crowned each hilltop. The two domes in this view are the 1806 Catholic Cathedral by Benjamin Henry Latrobe and the 1817 Unitarian Church by Maximilien Godefroy, both surviving. The graceful spire of Old St. Paul's Church, built in 1812 by Robert Cary Long Sr., burned in 1854. Robert Mills's Washington Monument, built between 1809 and 1829, now a very central place, marked the northern limit of development in 1850. (Courtesy of the Enoch Pratt Free Library.)

ANOTHER VIEW FROM FEDERAL HILL, 1850. East of Calvert Street, the center of town was already ceasing to be residential by 1850, and many of the best buildings disappeared within the next 10 years. The twin cupolas of the First Presbyterian Church, built 1791–1795, came down in 1860. The tall wooden spire of the German Reformed Church, 1803, held the town clock until its demolition in 1866. Only the great dome of Latrobe's Merchants' Exchange, 1815–1820, survived into the 20th century—just barely. (Courtesy of the Enoch Pratt Free Library.)

VIEW NORTHEAST FROM FEDERAL HILL, 1850. In 1975, East Baltimore, seen from the vantage point of Federal Hill, looked like a little port town on the Eastern Shore. It had grown since 1850 without changing in kind. The past five years have brought a change in kind. In 1850, the only visible construction site was President Street Station, the square pale building at center, now the Civil War Museum and quite invisible from Federal Hill. (Courtesy of the Enoch Pratt Free Library.)

VIEW DOWN THE HARBOR FROM FEDERAL HILL, c. 1900. By 1900, there had been shipyards at the foot of Federal Hill for 100 years. They were still there in the late 1970s, though schooners had given way to freighters. Only in the last generation has the working waterfront abandoned the Inner Harbor. Now, after 20 years of adjustment, million-dollar houses and condominiums rise from the Federal Hill piers, and most of the land in this view is on its way to becoming a prosperous residential district. (Courtesy of the Enoch Pratt Free Library.)

THE EAST END OF DOWNTOWN, 1903. Here is Baltimore's commercial heart on the eve of destruction by the Great Fire of 1904. The large buildings in the foreground are late-Victorian offices. Beyond them lies a dense-packed Dickensian dockland of the 18th and early 19th centuries. The Power Plant, built to power the city's streetcars and new when this picture was taken, is the sole survivor, though tall buildings make it invisible from the 1903 location. Today's downtown has more floor space and more light and air, though decidedly less mystery. (Courtesy of the Enoch Pratt Free Library.)

LOOKING SOUTHEAST FROM THE WASHINGTON MONUMENT, C. 1894. This rare view shows the last moment when something other than business dominated the skyline. The skyscraper would soon give artistic expression to private enterprise and turn skylines into collective cathedrals, but not until the second half of the 1890s. Here the dome of City Hall (1867) and the tower of the Post Office (1881) were the tallest structures south of the Washington Monument, and three-story houses covered every surface. Mount Vernon was still fashionable down to Saratoga Street. (Courtesy of the Enoch Pratt Free Library.)

LOOKING WEST FROM 10 LIGHT STREET, C. 1950.
When downtown rebuilt in 1904, the "burnt district" was still the wholesale center for the South, and hundreds of firms built relatively small buildings to store and sell bulk goods. This trade was largely gone by 1950, and much of downtown was going vacant. The Charles Center project (1955–1975) cleared 33 acres of 1904 buildings, closed streets, created "superblocks," and used the language of Modern architecture to proclaim downtown as a class-segregated office center. (Courtesy of the Enoch Pratt Free Library.)

THE HARBOR

THE BEGINNING, THE MIDDLE, THE APPARENTLY ENDLESS

PRATT STREET, 1890. Baltimore began at the Inner Harbor, and the Inner Harbor has always been the city's physical and business center. The port that began here in 1730 has spread for thousands of square miles, and the revival that began here in the 1970s is now following suit. The Inner Harbor has been through many changes. This picture was taken where Harborplace now stands. Global warming was far in the future as of 1890, and so were adequate bulkheads, so flooding occurred until after World War II. Try not to remember that Baltimore lacked a sewer system in 1890, and that the water in this picture was basically diluted sewage. (Courtesy of Lewis A. Beck.)

19

CONWAY STREET, C. 1900. Now a broad and glaring boulevard thronged with cars and visitors, Conway Street has always connected the harbor to Camden Yards. In the 19th century, that connection made it the ideal center for the Chesapeake tobacco trade. The State Tobacco Warehouses, on the left of this hogshead-filled picture, received freight by schooner; here tobacco was inspected by state officials and stamped, then sent on by rail or ocean-going ship. (Courtesy of J. E. Henry.)

THE MALTBY HOUSE, PRATT STREET, 1880. A little bit of Saratoga Springs near the Baltimore waterfront, the Maltby House welcomed shipborne visitors from just before the Civil War until the Great Fire of 1904. Here it watches over the festivities for the city's sesquicentennial in 1880. Note the difference in scale between the Victorian hotel and the earlier Georgian houses next door. Then imagine the difference of scale if the Maltby House had somehow survived until today. (Courtesy of Mrs. W. Irving Walker.)

200 West Pratt Street, c. 1910. This part of town was a quiet suburb in 1800 when Quaker merchant Moses Shepherd built his house at the corner of Pratt and Sharp Streets. Somehow Shepherd's house has survived, despite countless changes of use and buildings rising and falling around it. The long three-story building to its left, also a survivor, is approximately 60 years newer and was built for business. Urban renewal uncharacteristically spared these two, spoiling the look but animating the life of today's Pratt Street. (Collection of Lawrence H. Fowler.)

Pratt Street, 1908. Urban change happens continually. Here is Pratt Street, torn up for widening and new railroad tracks, in 1908. Ironically the whole area had been rebuilt within the preceding four years: it was all leveled in the Great Fire of 1904. (Courtesy of the Enoch Pratt Free Library.)

A Victorian Pratt Street Bridge. In 1868, after a murderous flood on the Jones Falls, the city called on Wendell Bollman, bridge-building genius of the Baltimore and Ohio Railroad, to build iron bridges that could withstand rushing water. Bollman's bridges remained in service until cars, not currents, grew too heavy for them. His Lombard Street bridge survives, high and dry, at the Baltimore Streetcar Museum. (Courtesy of the Enoch Pratt Free Library.)

A Classical Pratt Street Bridge. By 1922, Bollman's bridge, proud of its iron structure in an early Victorian way, was gone, and this smooth essay in classicism was carrying the added tonnages of cars and trucks. The large building at right is the Scarlett Seed Company, which survives, though in a very strange way. Look for it at the north end of the Scarlett Place Condominiums, built in the mid-1980s. (Courtesy of the Enoch Pratt Free Library.)

PRATT STREET, 1939. Dodging traffic on Pratt Street is nothing new. Jammed with wagons in the 19th century, Pratt Street was jammed with cars and trucks by 1939. At least now all the cars move in the same direction, and drivers have at least occasional views of the water. (Courtesy of the Enoch Pratt Free Library.)

DOWNTOWN

THE EPICENTER OF GROWTH, CHANGE, AND THE OCCASIONAL CATASTROPHE

DOWNTOWN AFTER THE GREAT FIRE, 1904. Here is Downtown after the Great Fire of February 1904. The fire burned for 36 hours and destroyed more than 1,500 buildings in the heart of the city. Virtually every corner of the original 1730 settlement was burnt over. The flames of 1904 were no respecters of architecture. They devoured honored Colonial survivors and brand-new skyscrapers. They claimed the proudest works of Baltimore's 19th-century architects, and suddenly Downtown, which had become something of an architectural palimpsest, was a clean slate for the architects of a new century. Baltimore's Great Fire, the first major city fire to occur in the age of portable cameras, gave the 20th century a preview of things to come. (Courtesy of the Maryland Historical Society.)

BALTIMORE STREET, 1850. Baltimore Street was Baltimore's only crosstown street for 100 years and was the city's main street for almost 200. In this 1850 lithograph, most Baltimore Street buildings were at least 50 years old, built for merchants who lived above the shops. Residents vacated their upper floors in the 1830s and 1840s to make room for workers and merchandise. Most of these small buildings would be gone within 10 years, victims of a needed revolution in architectural technology. (Courtesy of the Maryland Historical Society.)

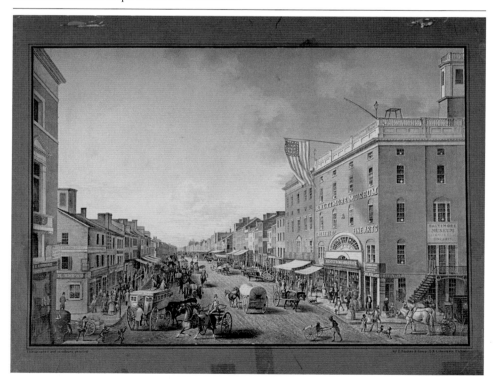

CARROLL HALL. Shown at the lower left of the Baltimore Street lithograph, Carroll Hall was designed in 1846 by Robert Cary Long Jr., one of the best architects in Baltimore's history. The meeting hall behind the large second-floor windows was frequently the site of raucous political and labor gatherings. A generous scale and an unusual mezzanine level gave Carroll Hall a curiously European look. Daniel Burnham's Continental Building replaced it in 1899 and survived gutting by the Great Fire in 1904. (Courtesy of the Enoch Pratt Free Library.)

GAY STREET, LOOKING SOUTH FROM ABOVE LEXINGTON STREET. Ugly Gay Street, which links Baltimore Street to the north, was beautiful in the first half of the 19th century. Most of the houses in this Civil War–era view date from around 1800, when the street was rich but diverse (African American painter Joshua Johnson lived here in 1801). William Strickland raised the sharp spire of Christ Episcopal Church in 1836. William Caldwell and William Reasin's Gothic Odd Fellows' Hall went up in stages between 1843 and, probably, the early 1860s. (Courtesy of the Enoch Pratt Free Library.)

THE SUN IRON BUILDING. Here is a real revolution in architecture, the world's first iron building and direct ancestor of every steel-framed skyscraper in the world. A. S. Abell, founder of the Baltimore *Sun*, brought iron pioneer James Bogardus down from New York in 1851. R. C. Hatfield and William Reasin gave Bogardus's engineering the look of a Venetian palace. Thin walls, open floors, and enormous windows kept the *Sun* happy here until it burned, or melted, in the Great Fire of 1904. (Courtesy of the Baltimore Camera Club.)

The American Building. It took a generation for the Baltimore *American,* Baltimore's second-biggest newspaper, to match the *Sun* in architectural magnificence, but Dixon and Carson's 1873 American Building surpassed its rival in vigor and ornament, if not in refinement. Here it is festooned—what other word fits?—for the sesquicentennial of 1880. The rival iron fronts, *Sun* and *American,* glared at each other across South Street for almost 30 years, until the Great Fire gave the American a chance to build a skyscraper. (Courtesy of the Enoch Pratt Free Library.)

SOUTH STREET, LOOKING NORTH FROM LOMBARD STREET, 1893. The revolution of iron construction allowed bigger buildings than ever before. By the Civil War, Baltimore's merchants had torn down large parts of the main business streets and replaced old brick Georgian buildings with new iron-fronted Italianate warehouses of four times the size. Here is South Street, the heart of the Victorian financial district, "the Wall Street of the South," showing how iron allowed Baltimoreans to give their city the romance of Renaissance Italy. (Courtesy of the Enoch Pratt Free Library.)

33–41 HOPKINS PLACE. Hopkins Place, a less desirable business location than South Street, adopted iron construction later and never became an all-iron street. By 1880, iron decoration was going out of style, and Hopkins Place was still being rebuilt. This picture captures the change in style. The building on the right uses iron for decoration, while those on the left sheathe their iron frames in brick. Look at the glossy paint on the iron columns. How many colors did Baltimore's iron facades have? (Courtesy of the Enoch Pratt Free Library.)

HANOVER STREET, LOOKING NORTH FROM PRATT. This picture catches the Victorian rebuilding of the Georgian city in mid-stride. The buildings at right are at least 50 years older than those at the corner. Buildings were smaller here than on more prominent streets but no less elaborate. As is often the case with buildings that disappeared in the Great Fire, the architects of these graceful structures are unknown. The discomforts of slogging through horse-fertilized slush, however, are easy to imagine. (Courtesy of the Enoch Pratt Free Library.)

SHARP STREET. Many businesses remained small and had no need for larger buildings. Thus many late-Georgian buildings like these, with small floors and brick bearing walls, were still going strong in 1880, when these owners and/or tenants went all out for Baltimore's 150th birthday. The alternation of survivals and replacements gave much of downtown considerable architectural variety. (Courtesy of the Enoch Pratt Free Library.)

LIGHT AND BALTIMORE STREETS, SOUTHEAST CORNER, c. 1906. After the 1904 fire, clearing and rebuilding began almost immediately. Sixty-eight architects opened new offices in Baltimore to capitalize on the opportunity. Most new buildings were at least vaguely classical, but there was no attempt to achieve uniformity—to say the least. This pair of buildings, individually good but oddly matched, lasted little more than two decades, yielding in 1929 to 10 Light Street, the greatest art deco skyscraper outside New York. (Courtesy of the Enoch Pratt Free Library.)

THE BALTIMORE SUN. Ambitious clients built ambitiously after the fire. The *Sun*, burned out of its pioneer iron front, moved three blocks west and commissioned this well-proportioned bit of Paris from Baldwin and Pennington, Baltimore's dominant late-Victorian firm. Abandoned by the *Sun* in the mid-1950s, it succumbed in the mid-1960s to Charles Center and John Johanson's Morris Mechanic Theatre, itself now abandoned. (Courtesy of the Baltimore Camera Club.)

REDWOOD STREET LOOKING EAST FROM HANOVER STREET. Here is a typical post-fire streetscape: restrained buildings of brick and stone with squarish outlines and squarish openings. Could the film-noir pedestrians in this 1938 photograph possibly have imagined that the hand of man, not fire, would sweep it all away again—and not just the buildings around them, but even the street pattern? All of the buildings in the foreground came down for Hopkins Plaza in Charles Center in the early 1960s. (Courtesy of the Enoch Pratt Free Library.)

MARKET PLACE LOOKING WEST ALONG WATER STREET. Center Market was the city's principal market for much of the 19th century. After the coming of mass transit, the Lexington Market became the dominant venue for family food shopping, and Center Market specialized in wholesale foods. The post-fire rebuilding gave form to this function. The city owned the wholesale markets in the foreground. Today's Port Discovery was the Fish Market. This picture gives a good sense of how remote Market Place felt from the skyscrapers of the financial district. (Courtesy of the Enoch Pratt Free Library.)

DOWNTOWN LOOKING WEST FROM THE CORNER OF LEXINGTON AND FRONT STREETS, 1932. Here is the power of a big American city. From left to right are Maryland Casualty (Simonson and Pietsch, 1911), now a parking lot; the Baltimore Trust Company, now 10 Light Street (Taylor and Fisher and Smith and May, 1929); the Munsey Building (Parker and Thomas, 1913), now apartments; and City Hall (George Frederick, 1867). Can you spot the giant blue bottle that crowned Joseph Evans Sperry's Bromo Seltzer tower from 1911 to 1932? Try finding the corner of Lexington and Front! (Courtesy of the *Evening Sun*.)

MERCHANTS' NATIONAL BANK. Buildings often survive and often disappear, but this one did both, and that is rare. Built in 1900 as an eight-story building, it lost its top six floors in the Great Fire of 1904. The big banking hall survived various tenants until, in 1983, it sprouted upper floors again—but with a difference! This is classic Post-Modernism from the 1980s. The curve in the Lombard Street front recalls a small building that the developers were unable to buy in time. (Courtesy of the Library of Congress, Prints and Photographs Division, Historic American Buildings Survey/Historic American Engineering Record.)

BALTIMORE STREET LOOKING WEST FROM THE JONES FALLS. Here is the east end of Baltimore's main street, probably in the 1880s. There was very little Victorian rebuilding at this end of the street, a sure sign that business was less intense here than farther west. Today's view shows the immense change in the city's scale and demonstrates that much of Baltimore's change has been progress, but note also how many small 1904 buildings survive at this end of the street. Business is still more intense farther west. (Courtesy of the Maryland Historical Society.)

ST. PAUL PLACE GARDENS. In 1917, James Preston, the most architecturally sensitive mayor in Baltimore's history, hired Carrere and Hastings to create a city-beautiful focal point for the expanding Downtown. Sadly Downtown has generally expanded in other directions, and Mayor Preston's gardens sit forlorn in the midst of traffic, but there is great sculpture here in the flowing steps and some drama in the ensemble. (Courtesy of the Enoch Pratt Free Library.)

CHAPTER 4

WESTSIDE

MUCH MORE THAN THE RETAIL CORE

HOWARD STREET SHOPPERS. Most Baltimoreans think of the Westside simply as the city's historic retail district. The new horse-car lines of the 1860s concentrated shoppers there, just as the Industrial Revolution gave them something to buy. The result, from about 1880 to about 1970, was a crowded big-city place full of scenes like this. Now that most Baltimoreans drive cars, the Westside has fewer shoppers and fewer shops. Its future will obviously be different—but then, its past was different, too. (Courtesy of the Maryland Historical Society.)

Dr. Thompson House, Southwest Corner of Lombard and Sharp Streets. Every city neighborhood was once a suburb, even Baltimore's Westside. This relaxed scene from the Civil War era looks more like Bolton Hill or Annapolis than a part of downtown Baltimore. The history of this residential enclave, already surrounded by commerce when this picture was taken, has never been studied in detail and obviously deserves to be. (Courtesy of the Enoch Pratt Free Library.)

FIRST BAPTIST CHURCH, "OLD RED TOP." Across Lombard Street from Dr. Thompson's house, in 1817, Robert Mills, architect of the Washington Monument, built this gem-like little pantheon for Baltimore's oldest Baptist congregation, a powerhouse group that numbered the Leverings and the Wilsons. This is great architecture, strong and refined at the same time. In the same year, Godefroy was raising a similar dome for the Unitarians at the corner of Charles and Franklin Streets. Baltimoreans could be Roman without being Catholic. (Courtesy of the Library of Congress, Prints and Photographs Division, Historic American Buildings Survey/Historic American Engineering Record.)

Three Tuns Tavern, Southwest Corner of Pratt and Paca Streets. Pre-railroad Baltimore depended on an endless flow of wagons bringing produce to market and returning with manufactured goods. By 1800, Baltimore was ringed with "farmers' hotels" like the Three Tuns, offering cheap lodging for man and stabling for beast. Unlike the fashionable hotels at the center of town, the farmers' hotels needed large lots for wagons, horses, and oxen. They were pre-industrial truck stops. A few remain. The Three Tuns, shown here in 1908, survived into the 1970s. (Courtesy of the Enoch Pratt Free Library.)

SOUTHWEST CORNER OF HOWARD AND SARATOGA STREETS. The Provident Savings Bank, designed in 1904 by Joseph Evans Sperry and now in use as a nightclub, is such a venerable landmark that it is hard to imagine it replacing other landmarks. But the Saratoga Hotel was already a century old when this picture was taken, and a year or two older when it went down for the Provident. Few pairs of pictures show better the broadening of architectural reference that occurred in the 19th century. (Courtesy of the Enoch Pratt Free Library.)

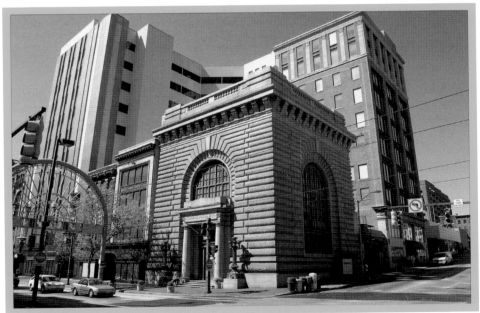

REDWOOD STREET LOOKING WEST FROM HOPKINS PLACE. Baltimore's Victorians loved the little off-center building at the corner of Liberty and German Streets, by then a touching reminder of the city's childhood. Few views capture so well the evolution of the city in the 19th century— from wooden town to brick Georgian city to iron-fronted Victorian metropolis. The Arena, described by Garry Wills as "the first Baltimore building that actually looked like an air conditioner," is a poor replacement for a necessary connecting street. (Courtesy of the Baltimore Camera Club.)

COMMERCIAL AND FARMERS' BANK. Mills Lane credits Benjamin Henry Latrobe and Maximilien Godefroy with the deceptively simple achievement of creating the first American public buildings that did not look like houses. Godefroy's beautiful little one-story bank of 1811 (the second story was added in 1882) met Lane's test and gave Baltimore its first chamfered corner à la francaise. The apsidal entrance and delicate sculptures were unprecedented, and contemporaries rated this bijou as highly as their largest and most expensive buildings. (Courtesy of the Library of Congress, Prints and Photographs Division, Historic American Buildings Survey/Historic American Engineering Record.)

SOUTHWEST CORNER OF HOWARD AND FAYETTE. By 1800, Howard Street was a solid half-mile of dealers who bought wheat from, and sold manufactured goods to, the farmers and rural storekeepers who stayed at places like the Three Tuns. Here are some typical Howard Street buildings of that era. By 1900, they stood wedged between garment lofts to the south and department stores to the north. Today the neighborhood is reviving briskly. The 21-story Centerpoint apartment tower stands at the site. (Courtesy of the Enoch Pratt Free Library.)

CHAPTER 5

NORTH CENTRAL

FASHION FOLLOWS CHARLES STREET

THE 1200 BLOCK OF NORTH CHARLES STREET. George Blake, who developed this row of large houses in the 1880s, was described as the first man who realized that Baltimore was big enough to have a great fashionable quarter on the model of Belgravia in London. This may be doubted; North Central Baltimore was already becoming a fashionable quarter before the War of 1812, a generation before Blake's birth. But we cannot doubt that North Central Baltimore was Baltimore's Belgravia until the First World War. The architecture of North Central, surviving and vanished, made it one of the greatest works of architecture and urbanism in American history. (Courtesy of the Maryland Historical Society.)

THE RECORD OFFICE AND COURT HOUSE. Lawyers often shape fashion, and the story of North Central Baltimore begins with the Court House. There have been three courthouses in Calvert Street since 1765. This view shows the 1805 version, designed by George Millman, at left. Robert Cary Long Jr.'s 1836 Record Office is at center, with Godefroy's 1813 Masonic Temple on the right. Wyatt and Nolting's 1894 Court House was the first American public building built in the new classical style of the Chicago World's Fair. (Courtesy of the Enoch Pratt Free Library.)

THE BATTLE MONUMENT AND MONUMENT SQUARE IN 1845. Here is America's first public monument, and here is Baltimore's first fashionable square. The houses are older than the monument—1800–1805 versus 1815—and show the power of courthouses to set fashion in early America. The pair of houses directly behind the monument is particularly fine, suggesting the work of some of the many French refugees who fled to Baltimore from revolutions in France and Haiti. The Court Square Building dates from 1927, the old Post Office from 1930. (Collection of the author.)

St. Paul Street Looking North to Saratoga Street. St. Paul Street, on the west side of the Court House, runs north along the kind of high ridge that people have always paid extra to live on. By 1812, this ridge was taking shape as a fashionable neighborhood of great charm. Why Baltimoreans destroyed this quintessentially Georgian environment in 1917, at the height of the Georgian Revival, remains a mystery. The large building on the left is the Athenaeum, built in 1847 by Robert Cary Long Jr. (Courtesy of the Library of Congress, Prints and Photographs Division, Historic American Buildings Survey/ Historic American Engineering Record.)

St. Paul Street Looking South to Saratoga Street. This detailed view shows the refinement and variety of which Baltimore's house builders were capable *c.* 1810. Long second-floor windows indicate upstairs drawing rooms. We still do not know enough to say whether these houses followed British fashions in this regard, or whether resident lawyers had their offices on the ground floor, less than a block from the Court House. (Courtesy of the Library of Congress, Prints and Photographs Division, Historic American Buildings Survey/Historic American Engineering Record.)

CHARLES STREET LOOKING NORTH FROM SARATOGA STREET. Charles Street runs the crest of the ridge and was tough to grade, but fashion was following Charles Street by 1820. If not Belgravia, this was certainly Baltimore's equivalent of Boston's Beacon Hill. This picture, taken in the 1870s, caught practically the last moment at which this stretch of Charles Street was uniformly residential. The Woman's Industrial Exchange, at the corner of Pleasant Street, built *c.* 1815 and altered many times, encapsulates the history of the block. (Courtesy of the Enoch Pratt Free Library.)

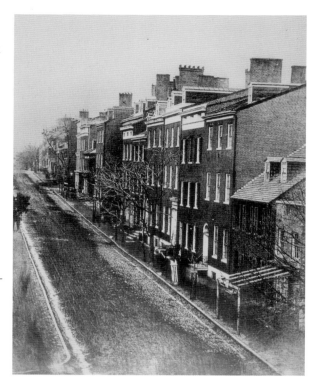

MULBERRY STREET LOOKING WEST FROM COURTLAND STREET. Pictures like this remind us that Baltimore was once a small city in the Middle Atlantic states, a place like Georgetown or Frederick. Even small houses had what Henry James called "a certain vividness of high decency . . . the real southern glow, yet with no southern looseness." Nowhere did they show to better advantage than on this steep slope, bulldozed in 1917 for Preston Gardens. (Courtesy of the Lawrence H. Fowler Collection.)

WILLIAM HOWARD HOUSE. William Howard, a son of John Eager Howard, was a skilled amateur architect. In 1829, two years after his father's death, he built Baltimore's first Greek Revival house, a rare Baltimore example of the temple form in domestic architecture, on a prominent Charles Street site across from Godefroy's First Unitarian Church. When Charles Street went commercial in the early 20th century, Howard's temple fell to an elegant furniture store by Baldwin and Pennington. This building survives as offices and elegant shops. Howard's four monolithic columns adorn a country house in Harford County. (Courtesy of the Library of Congress, Prints and Photographs Division, Historic American Buildings Survey/ Historic American Engineering Record.)

THE 500 BLOCK OF PARK AVENUE LOOKING SOUTH FROM CENTRE STREET. Temple-fronted houses like William Howard's were rare in Baltimore, even though Greek ideas flowed freely here. Like most big cities, where space was at a premium and front rooms needed light, Baltimore preferred to use Greek proportions and details within architectural forms that used space and light efficiently. The Anglo-American row house was a perfect medium, as witnessed by this dignified and harmonious block. Its destruction in the 1920s remains unavenged by great replacement architecture. (Courtesy of the Library of Congress, Prints and Photographs Division, Historic American Buildings Survey/ Historic American Engineering Record.)

THE 100 BLOCK OF WEST FRANKLIN STREET LOOKING WEST FROM CATHEDRAL STREET. This block of Franklin Street, built in the 1830s, was a dictionary of different ways to merge Greek elements into the Anglo-American brick tradition. The Lurman house, at center, with Greek pilasters and reception rooms on the second floor, was more a small palace than a large house. Cadoa Hall, to the right, was a rare Baltimore example of the English (and Bostonian) bow-front. The Frick house, left of the Lurman house, was less ordinary than it appears by comparison. (Courtesy of the Lawrence H. Fowler Collection.)

FRICK HOUSE ENTRANCE, 100 BLOCK OF WEST FRANKLIN STREET. Here is the splendor of Baltimore's Greek Revival, robust yet refined, executed all in marble as the base of a house that could have held up its head anywhere in the West End of London. Baltimore's reception of Greek architecture set the pattern for the later revivals of the 19th century: each revived style would find itself merged into the Anglo-American tradition of flat-fronted brick architecture. The modern entrance is part of Basilica Place. (Courtesy of the Lawrence H. Fowler Collection.)

WEST MOUNT VERNON PLACE AND THE WASHINGTON MONUMENT. What Franklin Street was for the 1830s, Mount Vernon Place was for the 1840s. By 1849, when this remarkable daguerreotype was taken, the four squares of Mount Vernon Place had been created and fenced, and splendid Greek Revival houses were under construction. Only Number 8, the five-bay house at center, survives unaltered. Note the construction in progress at Number 6. The dirt in the street at right center comes from digging the foundations of what is now Hackerman House. (Courtesy of the Maryland Historical Society.)

WEST MOUNT VERNON PLACE LOOKING WEST FROM THE WASHINGTON MONUMENT. Here again is Mount Vernon Place in its infancy. The Decatur Miller house, just right of Monument Street, was an early work of Niernsee and Neilson, the dominant Baltimore firm of the 1850s. Across the street, Louis Long's house for John W. Garrett, soon to be president of the Baltimore and Ohio, survived into the 1920s. The square itself, a simple grass plot here, acquired its third and current look in 1917, courtesy of Carrere and Hastings. (Courtesy of the Maryland Historical Society.)

BALTIMORE ACADEMY OF THE VISITATION. As the premier district of a regional capital, North Central Baltimore early attracted private boarding and day schools. This Catholic boarding school loomed above the 600 block of Park Avenue from the 1840s until its replacement by Greyhound bus buildings that are plainly too short for the site. With a large formal garden, the Visitation took up a full acre. (Courtesy of the Enoch Pratt Free Library.)

HOWARD STREET LOOKING NORTH FROM FRANKLIN STREET. Schools and culture went together. In 1873, after a downtown fire, several of the city's elite institutions settled on the west side of Howard Street, making it Baltimore's cultural center for two generations. Niernsee and Neilson's Academy of Music, the city's concert hall and opera house, dominates this picture. Edmund Lind's City College appears in the distance. The gabled building in the foreground, an indoor swimming pool called the Natatorium, was built in the 1880s. (Courtesy of the Enoch Pratt Free Library.)

THE 800 BLOCK OF CHARLES STREET. Charles Street was exclusively residential when it was new. Here is the refined classical carriage house of the Abell house, at the northwest corner of Charles and Madison Streets. Though the house survives, with a coffee shop on the ground floor and offices above, the garden and carriage house became unrecognizable after 1910. The square tower in the background is Emmanuel Church, unrecognizable now in its 1919 remodeling. (Courtesy of the Enoch Pratt Free Library.)

THE 900 AND 1000 BLOCKS OF CHARLES STREET. Charles Street has been so cut up that it is difficult to imagine it as a coherent architectural whole, much less as the most fashionable address in one of America's biggest and richest cities. Here is a taste of what we are missing. The year is 1939, and the houses in the foreground are being demolished for a moderne nightclub, still surviving. The houses north of Eager Street succumbed soon after to a less noble fate—surface parking. (Courtesy of the Enoch Pratt Free Library.)

UNION STATION. Built in 1873 as the flagship of the Northern Central Railroad, Union Station soon became part of the Pennsylvania Railroad, which built this French Renaissance chateau in the 1880s. Until then, it had been easier for Baltimoreans to go to St. Louis than to New York. With its porches and neatly tended gardens, this second Union Station must have seemed like a big, smoky Victorian country house in the middle of the city. The current station opened in 1911. (Courtesy of the Enoch Pratt Free Library.)

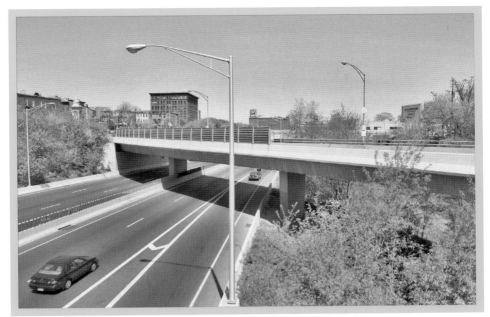

THE BIDDLE STREET BRIDGE. The Jones Falls valley has always been the back side of North Central Baltimore. There were water-powered mills here when the neighborhoods were farms. By the late 19th century, the Jones Falls ran in a pipe, and the valley carried Northern Central trains down to Calvert Street Station at the corner of Calvert and Franklin Streets. In this disorienting *c.* 1900 view looking north from the Chase Street Bridge, the house backs on the left belong to the 1200 block of Calvert Street. (Courtesy of the Enoch Pratt Free Library.)

NORTH AVENUE. No, this is not Mount Washington or Catonsville. North Avenue was an opulent semi-suburban boulevard in the second half of the 19th century, as these mid-century villas attest. They stood at the northwest corner of North and Maryland Avenues, overlooking a series of green parks called, collectively, Taney Place. This picture shows the start of demolition for the North Avenue market in the early 1920s. (Courtesy of the Enoch Pratt Free Library.)

TWENTIETH STREET LOOKING EAST FROM MARYLAND AVENUE. It may be hard to believe that North Avenue was ever suburban, but it is equally hard to believe that Twentieth Street, a block away, was ever urban. These houses, pictured in 1915, date from about 1870 and were part of a coherent city neighborhood that ran from Latrobe's cathedral to Thirty-third Street. Fashion followed Charles Street. Much has been lost, but enough survives for a successful reweaving. (Courtesy of the Enoch Pratt Free Library.)

BRYN MAWR SCHOOL. Founded in 1885, Bryn Mawr was a revolutionary experiment in education for girls. The founders went to New York for their architect, Henry Rutgers Marshall, whose Brearley School they much admired. Bryn Mawr moved out in 1931, and urban renewal destroyed both building and context. Bryn Mawr was one of a number of elite private schools that were located at the connection between North Central and Northwest in the late 19th century, drawing students from those two halves of fashionable Baltimore. (Courtesy of the Bryn Mawr School Archives.)

NORTHWEST

THE TURBULENT SEAS AROUND BOLTON HILL

BOLTON. Every city neighborhood was once a suburb, even Bolton Hill. This is Bolton, built in 1785, one of perhaps four dozen large villas that formed a "fox hunting belt" within a mile or two of Baltimore by 1800. Originally a 30-acre tract, Bolton was whittled away by development until, by 1850, it comprised exactly one square block at the joint between North Central and Northwest. Falling in 1901 for the 5th Regiment Armory, it gave its name to Bolton Hill, the best preserved of the Northwest neighborhoods. (Courtesy of the Maryland Historical Society.)

MOTHER SETON HOUSE AND ST. MARY'S SEMINARY. "A pretty Catholic town," wrote Chateaubriand of Baltimore in 1791, the year that French priests founded America's first seminary in open country near the young city. Today the little neighborhood of Seton Hill, around the old seminary walls, still has the feel of a pretty Georgian town. America's first native-born saint, Elizabeth Ann Seton, lived in the small house in the foreground. A lovely park makes up for the loss of Baldwin and Pennington's great Victorian seminary buildings. (Courtesy of the *Evening Sun*.)

THE 200 BLOCK OF WEST BIDDLE STREET. These houses were suburban when they were new in the early 19th century. They were integrated into the urban fabric within a generation, however, and made the connection between North Central and Northwest. "Biddle Street, once the abode of gentry," wrote the *Sun* in 1936, when this picture was taken to document their impending destruction for slum clearance and, 20 years later, state offices. But their genteel phase had long since set the tone for a genteel Northwest. (Courtesy of the Enoch Pratt Free Library.)

1000 McCulloh Street. This is not London after the Blitz, but it could be. America has never produced more London-like architecture than these houses from the early 1850s, nor has American decay ever looked so much like the work of the Luftwaffe as here in 1939. Note the long windows at the second-floor level: upstairs drawing rooms, a sure sign of genteel life with a staff of indoor servants. This neighborhood was demolished before it could acquire a name but was clearly the precursor of Bolton Hill. (Courtesy of the Enoch Pratt Free Library.)

221 WEST PRESTON STREET. The four-story London formula, with drawing rooms upstairs and dining rooms below, was rare in North Central and practically unknown in more modest neighborhoods, but it was for some reason very common in the Northwest neighborhoods in the years around 1850. It would be interesting to know why. Even narrow houses like these followed the London plan. Was the racetrack Baltimore's only Pimlico? (Courtesy of the Enoch Pratt Free Library.)

PRESTON STREET LOOKING EAST FROM MCCULLOH STREET. Baltimoreans have completely lost the memory of one of the greatest neighborhoods in their city. No trace remains of these distinguished houses, swept away for public housing as a slum clearance project in 1939, nor has anyone yet endeavored to reconstruct the lost world of this proto–Bolton Hill. Here is a good subject for a doctoral thesis! The bishops of the Episcopal Church lived near this corner for half a century. (Courtesy of the Enoch Pratt Free Library.)

HOFFMAN STREET LOOKING EAST FROM DRUID HILL AVENUE. Is it right to say that this variation on the London formula, oddly mixing the straight lintels of the Greek Revival with the heavy cornices of the Italian Renaissance, was unique in Baltimore? No one knows. No surviving examples remain, but there may have been others in the lost world of State Center and McCulloh homes. Baltimore's architectural history has enough interesting unanswered questions to launch 1,000 dissertations. (Courtesy of the Enoch Pratt Free Library.)

Preston Street Looking West from Park Avenue. The 5th Regiment Armory, which replaced Bolton in 1901, now stands in a moonscape of Modern architecture but was originally the centerpiece of a complete and living neighborhood. The church in the foreground was built in the same year, 1901—a sure sign that life was still going on and intended to go on. T. Buckler Ghequiere's design smacked of the 1880s and was very old-fashioned in 1901. It housed St. James Episcopal Church until 1927. (Courtesy of the Enoch Pratt Free Library.)

THE 200 BLOCK OF WEST HOFFMAN STREET. In 1912, when the Democrats nominated Woodrow Wilson in the 5th Regiment Armory, their shouting may have kept neighbors awake in this ambitious row of Renaissance houses from the Civil War era. (Courtesy of the *Evening Sun*.)

EUTAW PLACE, LOOKING SOUTH FROM WILSON STREET. Eutaw Place was laid out in 1856 as a trio of grass plots—"places," in the planning jargon of the time—in the middle of new blocks of Eutaw Street. In 1880, the decision was made to extend the street, with "places," to North Avenue, creating an avenue. Henry Blake, brother of Charles Street's George, built these spectacular rows in 1880 and 1881. Their demolition in the 1960s was a terrible loss, with terrible replacements. Can redevelopment bring revenge? (Courtesy of the Library of Congress, Prints and Photographs Division, Detroit Publishing Company Collection.)

THE ALTAMONT HOTEL. Some changes are for the better, and some are neutral, but the loss of the Altamont for a vacant lot, on the grandest boulevard in Victorian Baltimore, was and remains a pure loss. This corner cries out for a good building. The Altamont, designed by William Weber, was mainly a residential hotel: before cooking and cleaning became easy, single people lived in hotels or boarding houses and shared the cost of a cook and cleaning staff. (Courtesy of the Maryland Historical Society.)

LINDEN AVENUE LOOKING SOUTH FROM McMECHEN STREET. Even Bolton Hill itself, the rock that withstood the storm of urban renewal, has changed significantly. Witness Linden Avenue. Here is Linden Avenue in 1887: solid, respectable, and not yet complete (note the vacant lot in the right foreground). It looks like Bolton Street or McCulloh Street. Judged a slum in the 1960s, all this was swept away and replaced by Memorial Apartments, housing for the elderly. (Courtesy of the Maryland Historical Society.)

THE 1300 BLOCK OF McCULLOH STREET. Few Baltimoreans today would say that McCulloh Street is part of Bolton Hill, but it was and may be again when the curse of racism has lifted a bit further. The architecture west of Eutaw Place is the same as east of it—often better. Eutaw Place itself, now a dividing line, was originally the central boulevard of a rich neighborhood that was equally strong on both sides. Roland Avenue would repeat the pattern 40 years later. (Courtesy of the Enoch Pratt Free Library.)

GAIL HOUSE. What Ruxton and Sparks are today, Reservoir Hill was in the second half of the 19th century. This large Italianate villa of the 1850s combined urban and rural elements in a decidedly awkward way, but its romantic porch gave William Gail, a major tobacco merchant, sweeping views of the city and the harbor. The houses that replaced it in 1908 are now historic in their own right and stand on the front lines of Baltimore's neighborhood revival. (Courtesy of the Enoch Pratt Free Library.)

CHAPTER 7

MOVING OUT FROM THE CENTER

LOST WORLDS AND ALTERED LANDMARKS

GUILFORD AVENUE LOOKING SOUTH FROM CENTRE STREET. Baltimore is full of lost worlds. Sometimes the strangest bits of evidence recall them. Did you ever notice the tracks in Guilford Avenue? The romance of the iron horse is not what people expect to find in the shadow of Mount Vernon Place, but Guilford Avenue was a major rail center from the 1850s to the 1950s. The locomotive in this beautiful 1940 picture is emerging from Niernsee and Neilson's Calvert Station, the main depot of the Northern Central from 1855 until 1954, when the offices of the *Sun* replaced it. (Courtesy of the Enoch Pratt Free Library.)

THE 1100 BLOCK OF LAUREL STREET LOOKING EAST. Much of the city may once have looked like this. Eighteenth-century Baltimore, like Annapolis and Nantucket, had rows of wooden houses, a serious fire risk that the city outlawed in 1797. Laurel Street, now a lifeless back alley, seems to have been half-built when the law changed. Laurel Street was unusual only in surviving into the age of photography. The 1784 Friends Meeting House is at the end of this block, and the McKim Free School is around the corner. (Courtesy of the Lawrence H. Fowler Collection.)

507–511 South Caroline Street. Georgian Baltimore was not the Baltimore of John Waters, proud of its seediness. The young city, rough and violent as it was, aspired to be prim and proper, as these little gems attest. Note the columns, not pilasters, of the two door cases on center. This is full-dress architecture on a miniature scale. The vanished neighborhoods between downtown and Fells Point looked like this for block after block. (Courtesy of the Lawrence H. Fowler Collection)

Baltimore City Jail and Maryland State Penitentiary. As the Victorians fell in love with the Middle Ages and medieval architecture, the temptation to build dungeons in the style of donjons proved irresistible. Dixon, Balburnie, and Dixon designed the jail in 1857, and medieval stonework still symbolized incarceration when Jackson Gott designed the penitentiary in 1894. Gott's Romanesque "Pen" survives intact, to the delight of law-abiding citizens. Pieces of the jail remain. The new jail seems to symbolize years of idleness before an array of televisions. (Courtesy of the Enoch Pratt Free Library.)

CHURCH HOME AND HOSPITAL AND BROADWAY LOOKING NORTH FROM FAIRMOUNT AVENUE. As recently as five years ago, the old Church Home building (1839 and 1855) stood out jarringly in a landscape of Modernism, but tastes change—the lesson of this book. Today the people with power to shape the city are restoring surviving parts and re-creating vanished parts. Here is a fine example of ambitious re-creation. Every row house–scale building in the "now" picture is less than two years old. (Courtesy of the Enoch Pratt Free Library.)

UPTON, 811 WEST LANVALE STREET. Sometimes survival can be as odd and interesting as change. Upton began its life as a suburban villa in 1838, with superb views over the city. Like many a proud villa in Baltimore's history, it remained suburban for only about a generation. Row houses surrounded it by 1873, and it has gone through an astonishing variety of uses (including a radio station with antenna), but it is still there, intact, and serving a useful purpose for the school system. (Courtesy of the Library of Congress, Prints and Photographs Division, Detroit Publishing Company Collection.)

MOVING OUT FROM THE CENTER

CLIFTON HALL. This is the oddest survival story of them all. When the authors picked this photograph, they thought that this small-towny building could serve as a window to a vanished pre-urban world near Druid Hill Park. They had no idea that the building still survived, but here it is, then and now. Clifton Hall has sheltered everything from religious congregations to auto body shops—and another future appears to be in store, depending on who buys it. Not even authors know everything! (Courtesy of the Baltimore Camera Club.)

DISCOVER THOUSANDS OF LOCAL HISTORY BOOKS FEATURING MILLIONS OF VINTAGE IMAGES

Arcadia Publishing, the leading local history publisher in the United States, is committed to making history accessible and meaningful through publishing books that celebrate and preserve the heritage of America's people and places.

Find more books like this at
www.arcadiapublishing.com

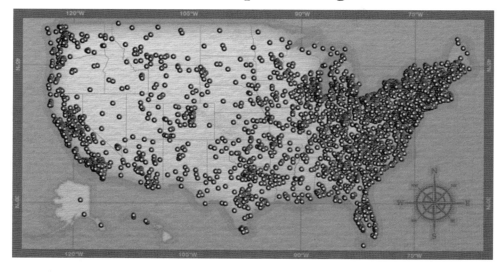

Search for your hometown history, your old stomping grounds, and even your favorite sports team.

Consistent with our mission to preserve history on a local level, this book was printed in South Carolina on American-made paper and manufactured entirely in the United States. Products carrying the accredited Forest Stewardship Council (FSC) label are printed on 100 percent FSC-certified paper.

MADE IN THE